11/18

KU-064-178

This book should be returned/renewed by the latest date shown above. Overdue items incur charges which prevent self-service renewals. Please contact the library.

**Wandsworth Libraries
24 hour Renewal Hotline
01159 293388
www.wandsworth.gov.uk**

Wandsworth

100 Ways To Be As Happy As Your Dog

Also by Celia Haddon

One Hundred Ways to Say I Love You

*One Hundred Secret Thoughts Cats
have about Humans*

*One Hundred Ways for a Cat
to Find Its Inner Kitten*

*One Hundred Ways for a Cat
to Train Its Human*

100 Ways To Be More Like Your Cat

100 Ways To Be As Happy As Your Dog

Canine Lessons for a Good Life

Celia Haddon

To Anna Wilkinson

First published in Great Britain in 2018 by Yellow Kite
An imprint of Hodder & Stoughton
An Hachette UK company

1

A CIP catalogue record for this title is available from the British Library

Hardback ISBN 978 1 473 68919 0
eBook ISBN 978 1 473 68921 3

Typeset in Celeste by Hewer Text UK Ltd, Edinburgh
Printed and bound in Great Britain by Clays Ltd, Elcograf S.p.A.

Hodder & Stoughton policy is to use papers that are natural, renewable
and recyclable products and made from wood grown in sustainable
forests. The logging and manufacturing processes are expected to
conform to the environmental regulations of the country of origin.

Yellow Kite
Hodder & Stoughton Ltd
Carmelite House
50 Victoria Embankment
London EC4Y 0DZ

www.yellowkitebooks.co.uk

Canine Ways to Live Happily

1.

Be loving

Your dog loves spontaneously and happily. He loves his human family. He loves his doggy friends. In his world, loving and being loved is what really matters. And that should be what really matters to us.

2.

Be optimistic and hopeful

———

See how your dog looks longingly at the food cupboard. She doesn't lose hope that you might, just might, give her a treat even if it is not her dinner time. An optimistic attitude to life makes the world seem a happier place to live in.

3.

Live in the present

Whatever your dog is doing, he is fully
involved with it. He lives in the now.
Keep your mind focused on what you are
doing at the moment. Don't let it stray
off into anxieties, obsessions or
resentments.

4.

Be genuine

When your dog licks your face, you know she means it. Dogs are emotionally straightforward. Being honest to yourself about what you really feel will help you handle your emotions, whatever they are.

5.

Accept the things you cannot change

———

Your dog doesn't rail at fate, simmer with resentments or moan that life is unfair. He knows that it is what it is. Accepting your life as it is, rather than fighting against fate, gives you time and energy to enjoy what can be enjoyed.

6.

Be sympathetic

Open yourself up to what others may be
feeling and be there for other people.
Your dog knows when you are feeling
unhappy and will try to comfort you. She
doesn't turn away from you when you
are in trouble. Instead she licks your
face.

7.

Keep life simple

——

Your dog is good at this. He likes food, walks, strokes, interesting smells, and chasing balls. He enjoys these one at a time. And he enjoys each one fully and absolutely. He doesn't waste energy complicating his life with over-thinking, over-committing, doing too much, or doing too many things at the same time. Dogs, unlike humans, do not multitask and are all the better for it.

8.

Don't let past misery prevent present happiness

Put aside past regrets, losses, hurts,
grievances, or failures. Bad things
happen to dogs, just as they do to
humans, but dogs are quick to leave the
past behind them and start again. Even
dogs that have been cruelly treated learn
to enjoy a new life when they are
rescued. Like them, move on.

9.

Look for the best in people

———

Your dog thinks you are wonderful and you respond well to that. If you seek out what is best in people, you are more likely to receive the best back.

10.

Don't let money run your life

———

Your dog lives happily without credit cards or bank accounts. He doesn't carry rolls of cash and he doesn't get into debt. Happiness doesn't depend on your bank balance.

11.

Be easily pleased

———

Your dog looks for ordinary stuff he will enjoy – lamp posts, crumbs on the kitchen floor, rabbit holes, sticks, or simply the pleasure of being near you. Look for the small pleasures of life and don't be too critical. You will enjoy life more.

12.

Don't worry about the future

___

Many of your worries will never happen.
Yes, sometimes your dog can be anxious,
but she is easily distracted by what is
going on *now*. She doesn't lie in her bed
at night mulling over future scenarios or
imaginary encounters. She goes to bed
and sleeps. Worrying about what might
happen tires the mind and doesn't help
ward off troubles.

13.

Don't sweat the small stuff

The day didn't go perfectly. Whenever did it? Your dog doesn't let little things upset him. He shakes them off and gets on with chasing his ball in the park.

14.

Stay curious and ask questions

—

Dogs are always investigating. On walks they are smelling and hearing and looking at the world around them. They will push their way into undergrowth or start digging a hole – to find out what is there. Being interested in your world is always good.

15.

Don't let dislike of others poison your life

___

Dogs can be best friends with bankers,
tax inspectors, dentists, politicians,
presidents, journalists, used-car salesmen
and traffic wardens.

16.

Leave your mark on your world

___

Your dog does this on lamp posts. We can do it by carrying out good work, volunteering, taking part in local activities, raising money for good causes, or helping the next generation. And by being a good friend to others around you. Like your dog.

Canine Ways to Work Happily

17.

Be a team player at work

———

Your dog is happy to team up with you
or another dog. Watch a team of huskies
racing through the snow or a pack of
wild dogs hunting together. Dogs know
that co-operation, rather than
competition, can work wonders. Value
teamwork over rivalry.

18.

Step up to the mark when something needs to be done

———

Dogs do their best to fight crime, rescue bomb victims, guard human buildings, and dig out earthquake victims. If dogs can help at moments of crisis, so can we. You may not be able to do everything when disaster strikes, but you can do something. So do it.

19.

Don't be afraid to ask for what you want

———

Dogs and humans work better for rewards. Your dog is very good at coaxing you into giving her food. She will put her head on one side, lift an imploring paw, give you a nose nudge or offer you melting looks. Paw-lifting or nose-nudging will not work for your boss, but a well set-out request might do the trick. Ask nicely and use charm, like your dog does.

20.

Don't let mistakes or failures get you down

——

Trial and error is the way dogs learn. Your dog doesn't go into a depression if something doesn't work for him. Mistakes are as useful as successes when you are learning a new skill. Knowing what not to do is as important as knowing what you should be doing. Use errors as tools for doing better next time.

21.

Ask for help

—

When your dog doesn't know what to do,
she looks at you to ask what to do next.
Dogs are relaxed about not knowing all
the answers. You should be, too. You
don't need to have all the answers.

22.

Don't give advice unless somebody asks for it

Dogs never give advice. This is one of the reasons why we get on so well with them.

23.

Be flexible

Your dog is always willing to have a go at a new game, eat something different or investigate something new. Don't be afraid to try new things, take on new ideas, or change your mind.

24.

Look at people's deeds, not their words

—

Sometimes the two don't match up. Your dog reads your mind by looking at what you do, not at what you say. She knows that words can mislead, but deeds don't. When colleagues or other workers talk the talk, keep an eye on whether they are also walking the walk.

25.

Be cheerful and willing

___

Guide dogs, sheep dogs, guard dogs,
search dogs and assistance dogs all enjoy
their work. Their cheerful willingness
makes them both reliable and valued.
Be like them.

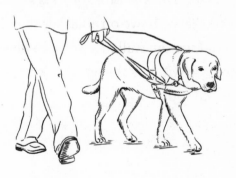

26.

You don't have to be top dog

Your dog fits into his place in the world.
He will happily follow you when you
lead. He doesn't mind taking orders from
you. He becomes part of a human–dog
partnership. And if he *is* top dog among
other dogs, he leads without
domineering or bullying. You can have a
happy life without always fighting to
come out top.

27.

Dogs don't talk

———

Learn from them the power of restraint
and the value of silence. When in doubt,
stay silent in the office canteen or in the
pub after work. Office gossip can
backfire on you.

28.

Don't work non-stop

Working dogs need regular rest and play sessions just as much as human workers do. Stopping work to rest or play will refresh your mind and body. Taking a break means working more effectively.

Canine Ways
to Have Fun

29.

Find fun wherever and whenever you can

——

Your dog has an endless capacity for fun and play. Puppies play. Old dogs play. Serious-minded sheepdogs play. Laid-back Labradors play. Tenacious terriers play. Dignified Great Danes play. Even cute little Chihuahuas play. Do it, too.

30.

Give a friendly greeting to people you meet

Your dog is good at this. Watch your dog making friends with other dogs. There's the run towards, pause, circle, and bottom sniff. Bottom sniffing is definitely not a good start to human friendship, but a friendly handshake and a smile will work well. Enhance your life by being friendly to people you meet casually during your day, like the delivery person, the shopkeeper or the receptionist.

31.

Walk on the funny side of the street

Your dog grins and she also makes a 'huff huff' noise, which is how she laughs. Opt for friends, films and books that make you laugh. Laugh and smile as often as you can.

32.

Goof around

—

Dogs are not self-conscious. Don't be self-conscious or stand on your dignity. Your dog loves having silly fun. Don't be afraid to play foolish games with your children or friends. Don't worry what others think. If *you* are enjoying clowning around, that's all that matters.

33.

Make time to stop and smell the roses

Your dog stops and sniffs whenever there is a scent that interests him. He sees life through his nose. We don't enjoy the same scents as he does, but we should not ignore the joy of scents that please us. Pay attention to the smell of flowers, newly mown grass, evergreen trees, good food, and newly washed laundry. Add these small joyful experiences to your life.

34·

Get outdoors and play ball games

——

Dogs play frisbee, flyball tracking, or just endless fetch. Humans enjoy cricket, football, netball, hockey, baseball, tennis, and many other ball games. Try one.

35.

Don't let mud, rain, snow or ice put you off having a good time outside

———

Muddy dogs are happy dogs. Watch your dog having fun paddling in a puddle! Enjoy getting dirty outside in the mud. What else are washing machines for?

36.

Try something new for fun

___

Modern dogs do agility, freestyle dancing
to music, tracking, shepherding, or nose
work. Try bungee jumping, pooh sticks,
pole dancing, winemaking, bridge,
birdwatching or some other new activity.

37.

Plenty in life is free

———

Your dog enjoys sunlight, rain, muddy
puddles, lamp posts, parks, fields, woods,
riversides, hills, mountains and beaches.
Most of these are free for humans, too,
though lamp posts do not have the same
allure for us.

38.

Go swimming

If there's a river or a pond near them,
dogs will plunge in and have a good
time. Then they shake water all over
their humans. Imitate them, except for
shaking off the water afterwards.

39.

Walk, don't drive

——

Dogs adore walkies – even dachshunds with short legs. The best way to stay fit is to leave the car behind and walk whenever possible. Walk to the office. Walk to the shops. It takes longer, but you see a lot of interesting things once you are outside in the street rather than shut away in the car, and your health benefits hugely.

40.

You don't need expensive toys for fun

———

Your dog has fun with a stick he has picked up on his walk. His favourite toys may be ragged, chewed or almost falling apart. He doesn't play with private jets, fancy cars, luxury yachts, or his very own helicopter. He doesn't need these things to enjoy himself.

41.

Play without needing to win

Big dogs handicap themselves when they play with small dogs, so as not to hurt them. Letting others win sometimes, makes them more likely to want to play next time. Take turns to win: dogs do.

42.

Take up hiking

Walk in the company of other people, or
simply you and your dog. Dogs like the
company of their people on walks and
the company of other dogs, too. Social
walking is particularly enjoyable for
people who live on their own.

*Canine Ways to
a Happy Home
and Family*

43.

Home is where loved ones are

Your dog would be happy in a bedsitter, a small flat, a canal boat, a caravan or a multi-room mansion, as long as you are there. To be with the right person is what matters most to her. Being with loved ones is what makes a happy home. You don't need five bedrooms, a snooker room, an indoor swimming pool, and garaging for six cars for happiness. You only need a place for people and your dog.

44.

Don't be too house proud

What is a bit of fur between friends?
Your dog doesn't care if a home is messy
or untidy. A comfortable home is better
than an immaculate one. Don't be a
crazed cleaner or a compulsive
redecorator.

45.

Play more with your family

___

Your dog plays with all her family companions – the cat, other dogs, or humans. The family that plays together stays together. Play, as well as the serious stuff, boosts bonding.

46.

Greet your family properly when you come home

———

Your dog listens for your footsteps and greets you with great affection and enthusiasm when you arrive home. A welcoming warm hug or kiss shouldn't be forgotten. Little loving things matter.

47.

Protect your home

———

Your dog has a strong sense of
belonging. He protects your home from
intruders and alerts you if he thinks
something is wrong. A home should be a
place of safety and relaxation for those
living in it. A few well-placed locks and
lights will add to your security. As does
your dog.

48.

Spend time with your family

Your time is the most precious thing you can give to children, partners and relatives. Your dog will watch TV with you, walk with you, go fishing with you, sit in the car with you, ramble with you, jog with you – even share your meal with you, if you let him. He is never far from your side. Just hanging out with your family shows them that you love them.

49.

Be willing to do your share of household chores

Dogs love fetching slippers, carrying home the newspapers, and picking up things on command. Service dogs help disabled people with shopping, with laundry, bringing the post and much more. Be as helpful as they are around the house.

50.

Be kind to children

—

Dogs are loving to their puppies.
Happiness is a warm puppy – and a
happy child.

51.

Ask for a hug if you would like one

You dog asks for your affection all the time. She leans against you, nudges you, brings you her toy, licks your hand, or puts a paw on your lap. There is no shame in asking for affection. It's all gain.

52.

Reward good behaviour and ignore bad behaviour in your family

---

Your dog learns best by this method. Punishment frightens dogs and makes it harder for them to concentrate on what they should learn. The same principles apply to family members. Train your family the dog training way, with love and rewards rather than criticism and punishments.

53·

Show, don't hide, your affection

——

Your dog does slobbery licks, thumps her tail, flops on her back, reverses her backside into you, or wriggles her whole body – to show her love. Remember to show your loved ones that you love them. Hugs and kisses are the currency of love. Do not take loved ones for granted.

54.

Share the sofa with others

Your dog likes to be close to you on the sofa, if you ask her up there. Piling up on the sofa with children, partners, or friends warms the heart. Friendly body contact with others, who enjoy it too, is another of life's pleasures.

55·

Be observing around family members

Dogs monitor what we are doing and notice our slightest actions. Don't miss the small clues that family members are unhappy or angry or stressed. Show that you care by noticing these signs and giving attention.

Canine Ways to
Happy Eating

56.

Enjoy your food

Dogs eat their dinner with enthusiasm. Food is more than merely fuel for living. Enjoyment of food is good for the digestion and good for your mood. It is part of a happy life.

57.

Never miss a meal

___

Your dog reminds you when it is her
meal time. Don't eat on the run. Take
time for a meal. Regular meals are better
for the digestion in both dogs and
humans.

58.

Eat what you are given

——

When other people are cooking for you, eat their food without fussing or complaining. Your dog will eat what is put before him and will also eat the same food uncomplainingly day after day, if that is what he gets. Be gracious to those who cook for you.

59.

Eat your greens

———

Your dog eats grass. She will also enjoy some fruit and some vegetables. Humans can eat a much wider variety of fruit and vegetables, so take advantage of that. Fruit and vegetables are important for human health.

60.

Eat well and sensibly

———

Your dog is not picky or faddy. Yes, allergies can be real for both dogs and humans and may need a special diet recommended by a doctor or a vet. But unnecessarily restrictive diets, or weird eating patterns, put you at risk of poor nutrition. Junk food is also bad for you.

61.

Leave a clean plate

___

Your dog licks her plate clean and always finishes up what she has been given. Don't waste food. Eat it all up. Give yourself a smaller portion, if you think you will have too much.

62.

Drink enough water

—

Dogs drink water all the time – especially in hot weather. They drink from dog bowls, rivers, puddles, and sometimes from the toilet if the seat cover isn't closed! Forget toilet water, but do make sure that you are drinking enough liquid throughout the day. Symptoms of dehydration include muscle cramps, headaches and irritability.

63.

Give new foods a little try

Your dog enjoys a change of diet, but sudden changes are bad for both dogs and for humans. Enjoy variations to your diet, but remember that drastically different ones may cause digestive difficulties. Or gas!

Canine Ways to Get on with Others

64.

Don't insist on being right, if you want to be loved

———

Your dog would rather be loved than be right, so he never argues back. He lets argumentative words go over his head.

65.

Be trustworthy with your friends

Your dog is always trustworthy. She does not gossip about you. Your secrets are safe with her. A friend's secrets should be safe with you, too.

66.

*Don't talk too much
or monopolise the
conversation*

———

Your dog doesn't spend his life with you
in constant talk. He is silent much of the
time. If you talk continually, you miss
hearing a lot of interesting things. You
cannot learn what you do not hear and
talking too much is disrespectful to
others.

67.

Be a good listener

—

One of the reasons you love your dog is that he is a very good listener and pays careful attention to you when you talk to him. You can tell him anything and he is never judgemental.

68.

Do not be racist

———

Your dog doesn't judge people by the colour of their skin. She is friendly to everybody, no matter what their ethnicity.

69.

Rejoice in another's success

Don't let envy spoil your happiness for others. Your dog shares in your happiness without feeling envious. He senses people's good moods and responds with his own. If you are happy, he is happy for you and with you.

70.

Don't be a moaner and a groaner

Dogs may yelp or whine when they are in pain or ill, but they don't complain or moan without good reason. Self-pity is very unattractive to others.

71.

Keep your opinions to yourself

———

Dogs do not have opinions about politics, religion, philosophy, or the state of the nation. They may have opinions about food, sex and smells, but they don't bore us with them or quarrel about them with other dogs. They will listen politely as we tell them our opinions and they never disagree with us. Strongly expressed opinions can weaken friendships.

72.

Make other people feel special

Your dog shows you how special you are
to her. Do the same to others. Remember
what matters to them and ask about it.
Send a birthday or a get-well card. Give
small thoughtful gifts, offers of help, or
just make time to listen.

73.

Do not be ageist

Your dog treats an elderly person with the same respect that he shows to a younger person. He greets them with the same friendliness. He does not blank them, write them off or patronise them. He knows that elderly people have a lot of love and friendship to give.

74.

Dogs forgive easily and often

They reconcile themselves with others after a falling out. Forgiveness is good for humans, too. If you forgive others, you let go of your anger and resentments, which would otherwise clog up your mind with bad feelings. Forgive others, let go of your anger, and move back into happiness.

75.

Practise kindness

———

Your dog is quick to comfort you when he senses that you are unhappy. Trained dogs guide blind people, aid deaf people, and do tasks for disabled people. Kindness to others is a path to happiness. Humans tend to be happy if they are kind, and to be kind if they are happy.

76.

Don't boast

Your dog doesn't need to brag about her abilities or her looks. She is confident enough to be modest. Self-satisfaction is unattractive and boasting about your possessions, your abilities, your spiritual achievements or your looks annoys others.

77.

Laugh with, not at other people

Your dog is good at making you laugh and he enjoys sharing the joke with you, even if he doesn't understand it. But he doesn't sneer or laugh at you, put you down, or make you feel bad.

Canine Ways to
Care for Yourself

78.

Exercise daily

—

Walk, run, jump, jog – whatever suits you. Your dog enjoys exercise. Even when she is old and arthritic, she will appreciate a gentle walk in the park. Choose exercise that is a pleasure not a chore, then you will do more of it.

79.

Do not risk becoming addicted

Dogs are good at sniffing out addictive drugs, but they never do more than that. They help police and customs officers find drugs, but they never use them.

80.

Meals, exercise and sleep should be as regular as possible

Your dog prefers her meals, her walks, and her sleeping times to be at the same time every day. A daily routine is the basis on which to build flexibility and creativity.

81.

Keep your anger under control

It is natural to be angry at times, but how you deal with it matters. Dogs growl first as a warning before they bite. Use words to express your anger, before shouting or hitting. Cool anger is more effective than rampant rage.

82.

Regular care of hair, nails and feet is good for humans and dogs

---

Your dog will groom herself in this way and she very much enjoys being brushed by you. It need not take hours, but daily grooming is part of human self-care.

83.

Brush your teeth regularly

——

Dogs clean their teeth by chewing bones or toys, or their owners clean their teeth for them using a doggy toothbrush. Clean teeth not only make breath smell sweet, but are important for general health in both humans and dogs.

84.

Have outside hobbies in your life

Your dog has hobbies like digging holes, burying bones, carrying stuff around, or chasing birds. Outside interests are a way of staying mentally alert.

85.

Regular check-ups maintain good health

___

Have your dog vaccinated and
checked-up yearly *before* he gets ill. Get
the same medical care for yourself. Your
health is as important as your dog's.

Canine Ways to Rest and Relax

86.

Get a good night's rest

───

Your dog doesn't stay up watching DVDs or box sets. And he doesn't play online games or do social media late into the night. A good night's rest is important to humans as well as dogs.

87.

Bedtime rituals are good for sleep

Your dog turns in a circle before lying down to sleep. Familiar rituals before getting into bed, like silencing your mobile, brushing your teeth, or reading a favourite book, will help you get into the mood for a good night's sleep.

88.

Wake up and stretch

———

Your dog stretches once or twice when she leaves her bed. Many dogs and humans are stiff when they have been sleeping. A simple stretch or two helps to start the day well.

89.

Take a power nap

——

When you've not had enough sleep
lately, or when there is a bit of spare
time, take a daytime nap. It's better for
you than a caffeine boost. Your dog naps
a lot during the day, when there is not
much else for him to do. It is a good use
of time for busy people.

90.

Seek warmth for relaxation

———

Dogs enjoy a warm kitchen, a roaring log fire, or the pleasure of good central heating. Warmth, whether it comes from a radiator, an extra sweater, or from the sun itself, helps dogs and humans relax.

91.

Learn the art of doing nothing very much

—

Dogs laze around or sleep when there's not much else to do. It's a way of saving energy for when you need it. Don't feel you have to fill up time with constant busyness. Taking it easy is not a waste of time.

Canine Ways to
Happy Attitudes

92.

Live large . . . even if you are small

———

It is your attitudes that matter most for your happiness. Your dog doesn't let his size determine his life. Small dogs have as much energy and enthusiasm as large dogs. A tiny terrier often has the heart of a lion.

93.

Choose experiences over stuff

———

Shopping is not a recreation that your dog enjoys. She would prefer a good walk rather than shopping for a new collar. Shop for what you need, not what you want. You do not need diamond necklaces, designer watches, expensive handbags or luxury shoes to be happy.

94.

Don't be a snob or condescend to others

The next-door poodle's pedigree means nothing to your dog. What he looks for in other dogs is playfulness and goodwill, not the right social status. Be friendly to other people whatever their looks, income or intellectual ability. You will have more friends that way.

95.

Learn something new

—

Your old dog can learn new tricks and
will enjoy doing so. Learning to dance,
bookbinding, painting classes, card
games, or taking courses, are all ways to
ward off old age and enrich your life.
You are never too old to learn.

96.

Your deeds are more important than your looks

———

Handsome is as handsome does. Your dog doesn't worry about how he looks. Scruffy mongrels or weird-looking crossbreeds have as much joy in life as any dog that wins at Crufts dog show. Dogs are not vain, neither should you be.

97.

Cultivate contentment

—

Your dog adjusts to her life and enjoys
what she has. She isn't jealous if other
dogs have bigger beds, more expensive
collars or richer owners. She is content
with proper meals, warm beds, regular
walks and a loving owner. Wanting what
you do not or cannot have is a way to
make yourself miserable.

98.

Live by your own standards, not by other people's

———

Your dog isn't fussed about what others think when he scratches an itch, pursues a possible flea, barfs on the carpet, or sniffs your visitor in an embarrassing way. You may be disconcerted by his behaviour, but he is not discombobulated at all. Do your own thing without worrying about what others think.

99.

Do whatever you do with all your might

Your dog does everything with great eagerness, whether it is eating, walking, greeting, or performing tricks. If somebody throws a ball for her, she responds as fervently for the twentieth time as for the first. Imitate her enthusiasm.

100.

*Be the person your
dog thinks you are*

———

Your dog looks up to you, enjoys your
company, forgives your blunders, and
loves you dearly. He thinks you are
wonderful. Be wonderful.

Visit Celia Haddon's website
www.celiahaddon.com
for useful advice about cats and other
small animals.

She can be found on Facebook at
www.facebook.com/CeliaHaddonBooks

Her cat, George, blogs at
george-online.blogspot.co.uk